BLOODTHIRSTY PLANTS

AN IMAGINATION LIBRARY SERIES

SUNDEWS
A Sweet and Sticky Death

By Victor Gentle

With special thanks to the people at
the Carolina Biological Supply Company
and Peter Paul's Nursery,
and to Mr. Isao Takai,
for their kind encouragement and help.

Gareth Stevens Publishing
MILWAUKEE

For a free color catalog describing Gareth Stevens' list of high-quality books and multimedia programs, call 1-800-542-2595 (USA) or 1-800-461-9120 (Canada). Gareth Stevens Publishing's Fax: (414) 225-0377. See our catalog, too, on the World Wide Web: http://gsinc.com

Library of Congress Cataloging-in-Publication Data

Gentle, Victor.
  Sundews: a sweet and sticky death / by Victor Gentle.
    p. cm. — (Bloodthirsty plants)
  Includes bibliographical references (p. 23) and index.
  Summary: Introduces these carnivorous plants by describing their traps, plant types, diet, and nutrient-poor habitats with the consequent benefit of carnivory.
    ISBN 0-8368-1658-7 (lib. bdg.)
    1. Sundews–Juvenile literature. [1. Sundews 2. Carnivorous plants.] I. Title. II. Series: Gentle, Victor. Bloodthirsty plants.
  QK495.D76G46   1996
  583'.121–dc20   96-5606

First published in 1996 by
Gareth Stevens Publishing
1555 North RiverCenter Drive, Suite 201
Milwaukee, WI 53212 USA

Text: Victor Gentle
Page layout: Victor Gentle and Karen Knutson
Cover design: Karen Knutson
Photo credits: Cover (main), p. 5 © Ken Davis/Tom Stack & Associates; cover (background) © Stuart Wasserman/Picture Perfect; p. 7 © Rod Planck/Tom Stack & Associates; p. 9 © Larry West; p. 11 © Visuals Unlimited/J. Alcoch; pp. 13, 15 © David M. Stone 1983/PHOTO/NATS; p. 17 © Patricia Pietropaolo/Peter Paul's Nursery; p. 19 © Isao Takai; p. 21 © Visuals Unlimited/H. A. Miller 1978

Printed in the United States of America

1 2 3 4 5 6 7 8 9 01 00 99 98 97 96

TABLE OF CONTENTS

A DAMSELFLY FOR DINNER

A brilliant blue damselfly flits from flower to flower. Aloft again, it catches the scent of nectar and sees a glistening plant that looks a little like a red-speckled catherine wheel. It flies toward the sweet smell. Once it lands, the damselfly is stuck fast to a sticky **tentacle**.

Nearby, other tentacles start to ooze more sticky liquid. They bend toward the insect. A brief struggle, and the damselfly's legs, wings, and body are hopelessly trapped. Another meal is ready for the sundew.

Sundews are members of a unique plant group: **carnivorous** plants — plants that eat animals.

A damselfly stuck on a sundew plant. Attracted by the sundew's glistening, sweet-smelling droplets, many insects are lured to their death.

HOW TO MAKE INSECT SOUP

Within a short time of a catch, the sundew leaves are in motion – *slow* motion. No need to hurry. That insect isn't going anywhere. More sticky juices seep out through the tentacles that reach for the insect. The leaves of some sundew plants also curl slowly around their victims.

The juices that cover the insect contain an **acid** and **enzymes** that **dissolve** all the soft parts of the insect. These parts provide food for the plant. This "insect soup" is sucked back into the plant by the same tentacles that made the sticky juices in the first place.

The hard parts of the insect, its **exoskeleton** and its wings, are not eaten. They will drop to the ground later.

A close-up view (24 times life size) of the droplets on a round-leaved sundew, *Drosera rotundifolia* (DROSS-er-uh roe-TUN-di-FOE-lyuh).

THEY CATCH THEIR OWN FERTILIZER

Many sundews grow in constantly wet conditions in poor soil. Others have adapted to survive periods of hot, dry weather.

Either way, they need to eat insects to survive. Poor soil can't give the sundews all the **nutrients** they need. But insect bodies are rich in exactly those nutrients.

By catching their own **fertilizer**, sundews have an advantage that other plants don't have.

An ichneumon (ik-NEW-mun) wasp trapped in a round-leaved sundew. This common sundew grows in Canada, the northern United States, Asia, and Europe.

WHERE IN THE WORLD . . . ?

Every continent in the world except Antarctica is home to sundews. Sundews grow in almost any climate, from the lakes and swamps of North America to the jungles of Brazil; from the snowy mountains of Scandinavia to the warm, dry plains of Australia.

More than a hundred **species** of sundews live on our planet. More than half of these species live in Australia.

The redink sundew from southwestern Australia. These sundews grow in drier climates than most other sundews.

ALL SHAPES, SIZES, AND COLORS

The **genus**, or group, name for all sundews, except for the Portuguese sundew, is *Drosera* (DROSS-er-uh).

Sundews come in all shapes and sizes. The smallest sundew species is only about .4 inch (1 centimeter) wide. The largest grows 5 feet (1.5 meters) high. Leaves may be round, spoon-shaped, long and spindly, or pear-shaped.

The delicate flowers of sundews range from white, to pink, to brilliant red or purple. Some sundews have metallic orange flowers, and others have bright yellow ones.

The tentacled leaves are usually green or red or greenish yellow. And boy, are they hungry!

The threadleaf sundew *Drosera filiformis* (fil-ee-FOR-miss) with a newly caught dragonfly and the remains of many other insects.

THAT'S QUITE A DIET!

Depending on the size of the sundew, snacks can range from the smallest of flying insects, such as midges and fruit flies, to larger flies, butterflies, mosquitoes, and moths. Sundews even eat dragonflies, millipedes, centipedes, and spiders.

One collector provided a **colony** of fruit flies to his new threadleaf sundew *Drosera filiformis* (DROSS-er-uh filli-FORM-iss). Within a week, the entire colony of fruit flies had been consumed by the sundew. Every one of the sticky, spindly leaves was black, covered with fruit flies.

This threadleaf sundew from Cape Cod, Massachusetts, has caught a skipper moth.

THE PORTUGUESE SUNDEW

The Portuguese sundew is the only species in the genus *Drosophyllum*. Its full name is *Drosophyllum lusitanicum* (druh-SOFF-ill-um loo-sih-TAN-ik-um).

Unlike most of its cousins in the *Drosera* genus, the Portuguese sundew prefers dry, stony soils. It lives in Portugal, Spain, and Morocco. Like the *Drosera* sundews, its leaves are covered with hundreds of small, sticky tentacles. The Portuguese sundew's leaves do not curl around its **prey**. Instead, the insects are smothered in the sticky digestive juices.

Small flying insects like mosquitoes and midges are attracted by the honey-like smell of the ooze on its tentacles.

A Portuguese sundew plant. In the wild, during the dry season, these plants get the moisture they need from dew and fog.

THE RAINBOW PLANT

The other genus of sticky-tentacled plants is *Byblis* (BIB-liss).

There are only two species, both commonly called rainbow plants.

Byblis gigantea (BIB-liss jigg-un-TAY-uh) grows in southwestern Australia.

Byblis liniflora (BIB-liss linni-FLOR-uh) grows in parts of northern Australia and in New Guinea.

Large moths, mosquitoes, grasshoppers, and flies are among the wide variety of live snacks these plants catch for themselves.

The simple but beautiful flower of a rainbow plant from Australia. During dry seasons, the plants die back and grow again either from seed or from roots that have survived.

FROM SPRING TRAPS TO DEATH PITS

Sundews catch their prey on sticky tentacles. Other carnivorous plants use different "tricks of the trade."

Venus fly traps catch insects with incredibly fast spring traps. Pitcher plants catch insects, small birds, mice, frogs, and even small monkeys in deadly pitfall traps. Other carnivorous plants, the butterworts, catch their prey on greasy, oozing leaves. Yet others, the bladderworts, act like midget vacuum cleaners, sucking in small insects and tiny fish. Some carnivorous **fungi** even lasso their prey!

You can learn more about the strange and wonderful world of carnivorous plants by reading other books. You can also learn more by getting your own plants and watching them grow.

It is not unusual to find more than one kind of carnivorous plant growing in the same area. Here, threadleaf sundews grow side by side with trumpet pitchers.

GROWING SUNDEW PLANTS

Sundews are the easiest of all carnivorous plants to grow. Like most other carnivorous plants, they need **humid** conditions and plenty of water. After all, they must keep making nectar and digestive juices for their sticky tentacles. Keep a partially open cover on your growing container to keep the **humidity** level high. Get ideas and directions from the people who supply you with the plants.

WHERE TO GET PLANTS OR SEEDS

Here are some addresses of carnivorous plant suppliers. For other sources, contact a club or society listed on the next page.

Heldon Nurseries
Ashbourne Road
Spath Uttoxeter, ST14 5AD
England

Carolina Biological Supply Company
2700 York Road
Burlington, NC 27215 USA

Peter Paul's Nursery
4665 Chapin Road
Canandaigua, NY 14424 USA

Exotica Plants
Community Mail Bag
Cordalba, QLD 4660
Australia

Hillier Water Gardens
Box 662, Qualicum Beach
BC V9K 1T2
Canada

Silverhill Seeds
P.O. Box 53108, Kenilworth 7745
Republic of South Africa

MORE TO READ AND VIEW

Books (nonfiction):   *Bladderworts: Trapdoors to Oblivion.* Victor Gentle (Gareth Stevens)
Butterworts: Greasy Cups of Death. Victor Gentle (Gareth Stevens)
Carnivorous Mushrooms: Lassoing Their Prey? Victor Gentle (Gareth Stevens)
Carnivorous Plants. Nancy J. Nielsen (Franklin Watts)
Killer Plants. Mycol Doyle (Lowell House Juvenile)
Pitcher Plants: The Elegant Insect Traps. Carol Lerner (Morrow)
Pitcher Plants: Slippery Pits of No Escape. Victor Gentle (Gareth Stevens)
Plants of Prey. Densey Clyne (Gareth Stevens)
Venus Fly Traps and Waterwheels. Victor Gentle (Gareth Stevens)

Books (fiction):   *Elizabite: Adventures of a Carnivorous Plant.* H.A. Rey (Linnet)
Island of Doom. Richard Brightfield (Gareth Stevens)

Videos (nonfiction): *Carnivorous Plants.* (Oxford Scientific Films)

Videos (fiction):   *The Day of the Triffids* and *The Little Shop of Horrors* are fun to watch.

WHERE TO WRITE TO FIND OUT MORE

Your community may have a local chapter of a carnivorous plant society. Try looking it up in the telephone directory. Or contact one of the following national organizations:

Australia
Australian Carnivorous Plant Society, Inc.
P.O. Box 391
St. Agnes, South Australia 5097 Australia

New Zealand
New Zealand Carnivorous Plant Society
P.O. Box 21-381, Henderson
Auckland, New Zealand

United Kingdom
The Carnivorous Plant Society
174 Baldwins Lane, Croxley Green
Hertfordshire WD3 3LQ
England

Canada
Eastern Carnivorous Plant Society
Dionaea, 23 Cherryhill Drive
Grimsby, Ontario, Canada L3M 3B3

South Africa – has no CP society, but
a supplier to contact is:
Eric Green, 11 Wepener Street
Southfield, 7800, Cape, South Africa

United States
International Carnivorous Plant Society
Fullerton Arboretum
California State University at Fullerton
Fullerton, CA 92634 USA

If you are on the Internet, or otherwise on-line, you can call up a World Wide Web page that gives links to other Web pages of interest to carnivorous plant enthusiasts: http://www.cvp.com/feedme/links.html

GLOSSARY

You can find these words on the pages listed. Reading a word in a sentence helps you understand it even better.

acid (ASS-id) — a harsh liquid that can dissolve many things 6

carnivorous (kar-NIV-er-us) — flesh-eating 4, 20

colony (KAH-luh-nee) — a group of animals, plants, or other organisms that live together 14

dissolve (dih-ZOHLV) — to make into a solution or fluid 6

enzymes (EN-zimes) — special substances that help digestion 6

exoskeleton (EK-so-SKEL-uh-tun) — the hard outer casing of insects 6

fertilizer (FER-tuh-LIE-zer) — a substance that helps plants grow 8

fungi (FUN-JYE) — the plural of **fungus** — a fungus is a kind of plant that has none of the special green substance you can see in most leafy plants, so it can't make its own food from sunlight, air, and water 20

genus (JEE-nus) — a group of closely related plants or animals 12, 16, 18

humid (HYOO-mid) — damp 22

humidity (hyoo-MID-uh-tee) — dampness in the air 22

nutrients (NOO-tree-unts) — substances with good food value 8

prey (PRAY) — a victim of a hunter, trapper, or trap 16, 20

species (SPEE-shees) — an individual type of plant or animal 10, 12, 16, 18

tentacle (TEN-tuh-kull) — a small hairlike arm out of which oozes a sundew's sticky liquid 4, 6, 12, 16, 18, 20, 22

INDEX